Journey to Success
The "Unforgotten" Teen

(All the Things You Don't Get Taught)

ERICA M. ODOM

WestBow Press books may be ordered through booksellers or by contacting:

WestBow Press
A Division of Thomas Nelson & Zondervan
1663 Liberty Drive
Bloomington, IN 47403
www.westbowpress.com
844-714-3454

ISBN: 979-8-3850-0779-0 (sc)
ISBN: 979-8-3850-0780-6 (e)

Library of Congress Control Number: 2023917783

Print information available on the last page.

WestBow Press rev. date: 09/22/2023

WestBow
PRESS®
A DIVISION OF THOMAS NELSON
& ZONDERVAN

To my nephews, TJ and Tyreese, and niece, A'reazon. You are the future of this family. I am determined for you all to have a future of wealth and limitless opportunities. You all are the reason why I go so hard.

A winner is a dreamer that never gives up.
—Nelson Mandela

Contents

Preparing for the Journey
(Module 1)

On Your Journey ...

When you earn and/or receive money currently, do you save some of the money or do you spend it all?

_____

_____

_____

Do you have a savings or checking account?

_____

_____

_____

Do you have at least two ways in which you generate income (e.g., mow lawns, work, and babysit)?

_____

_____

_____

Reflection Time

Why Do We Need Financial Skills?

_____

_____

_____

_____

_____

Being financially literate is one piece to the puzzle, but having the vision and correct mindset are just as important. Let's get started.

A *vision board* is a tool utilized to write down your visions and/or dreams you aspire to accomplish in your life. We all have visions and dreams, but the first step is writing them down. This provides clarity and focus and is the beginning to bringing your vision to life. It is no good for us to keep visions only in our minds. We need to write them down.

Success task: Fill in each square with a different goal or dream you want to achieve some day. With this activity, remember to dream *big*, not small! Your board can be updated or changed at any time.

What's Your Vision?

Who Are You?

Question: What's the difference between the rich and poor?
Answer: Mindset.

Poor

focused on looking rich

waiting on someone to come and save them

buys beyond their means

uses credit because they don't have cash

carries a balance on credit cards

no money management skills

Rich

focused on being rich

buys luxury after they hit their money goal

buys within their means

have financial goals

teaches themselves financial literacy

relies on only themselves

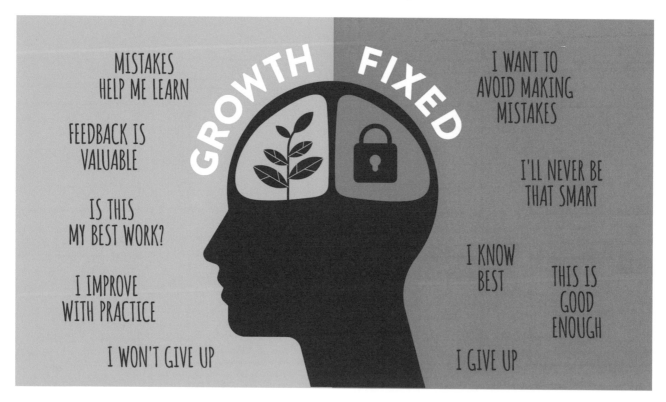

Wants versus Needs

Wants are things we don't really need to have in life, such as electronics, expensive jewelry, and going on vacations.

Needs are items that are necessary for us to have, such as housing, food, medications, and clothing.

Financial Literacy 101

What Is Financial Literacy?

Financial literacy is being able to use your skills and knowledge to manage your personal finances in areas, such as savings, budgeting, credit, and investments.

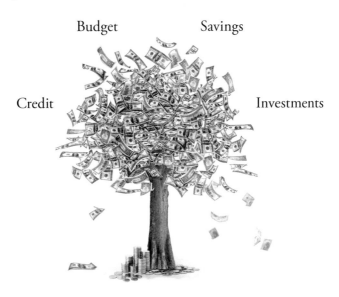

Benefits of Having a Financial Literacy Skill Set
- do the things you enjoy in life
- accrued savings for emergencies
- income to start a business
- build generational wealth

Money is a medium exchange that comes in the form of coins and bills. It allows people and businesses to pay for goods and services. Money can look different in other countries and governments outside the United States. It's most important to note that money is a tool that is available for people to use. Having personal financial control requires you to be aware of what money you have coming in and what money you have going out.

Money Going Out   Money Coming In

Money is broken down into four categories based on how we spend.

Four Uses of Cash

U Unexpected Expenses and Emergencies

Every person at least once in their life span will experience a time when they have to pay for something they didn't plan for.

Examples: job loss, unplanned medical bills, home repairs, auto repairs.

S Specific Short-Term Savings Goals

Being financially literate is knowing how to save for specific things we want to do and being properly prepared to pay for those things.

Examples: vacations, wedding, new car, a home.

E Everyday Spending

In life we have what we call necessities—items necessary for us to spend money on.

Examples: groceries, utilities, rent, entertainment, gas, bills, debts.

S Sources of Investment

Contributing money to some sort of investment is key. Your money should always be working for you by generating and building more money (wealth) for you.

Examples: real estate, stocks, bonds, business income.

How to Begin Saving 101

When most people hear about savings, they ultimately think of money they have in their bank account. Well, when you think of savings, you should think of the term *emergency fund*. An *emergency fund* is money set aside in the event someone needs it for an unexpected expense or emergency.

Smart Strategies

- Have smart spending habits.
- Don't spend all the money you earn or receive.
- Put money in your emergency fund.
- Open a savings account.
- Understand that money is a tool ("Four Uses of Cash").
- Try not to owe anyone, but if you do, pay them back quickly.

The Piggy Method

The piggy method is a budgeting system that was created to help you learn how to save. Follow the steps below to begin your journey to saving.

Items needed: Sharpie, empty jars with lids, three sheets of paper, and tape.
Step 1: Find four empty jars around your house.
Step 2: Cut your paper into four squares.
Step 3: Label each square using the Sharpie and tape each square to a jar.
Step 4: Label each jar.

Jar 1: Penny Fund
Every time you get a penny, drop it into this jar. Save as many pennies as you can until the jar is completely full. Once the jar is full, take it to the bank and cash in the pennies. Take the money earned from this jar and add it to any of the jars you choose. Start the process over again.

Jar 2: Emergency Fund
If you are working, you should aim to save a set dollar amount per paycheck. If you have a bank account, set up your direct deposit whereby the amount you will save per check or month will go directly into your savings account and the remainder of your check goes into your checking account.
Note: If you are not working, every time you earn or receive money, you should still aim to save something! Don't spend it all. Remember emergencies will happen.

Jar 3: Fun Fund
We must pay ourselves first. When we receive money, it is only right that we do something we want or purchase something we have been wanting. It's for fun, just like it sounds! Just remember not to overdo it and spend too much.

Jar 4: Purchase Fund
This fund is a specific short-term savings. As mentioned earlier, in the "Four Uses of Cash," one way we spend money is by saving for something specific. Use this fund to save specifically for something you want to purchase. Maybe it's a video game, a pair of shoes, or an outfit. Save until you have enough money to purchase what you want, and then start the process over again.

On the second sheet of paper, track monthly how much money each jar contains. Remember to track when you make deductions from jars too. This sheet is like your bank statement tracking each jar.

Success Check-In

Which fund in the piggy method is working well for you?

_____

Which fund in the piggy method is not working well? Why?

_____

Notes

_____

_____

_____

_____

Fundamental Basic Financial Skills 101

Basic Necessities Checklist

Checking and Savings Account

When we talk about building wealth for ourselves and placing ourselves in a healthy financial position that comes with making smarter choices and decisions, it makes no sense to have to find a place to go and cash your paycheck. Needing to find a store to cash your check can potentially come with standing in long lines and having to pay a fee. That fee can range from 1 percent to 12 percent of the value of the check amount. Having a checking account or savings account allows you to receive your paycheck at no additional cost.

As mentioned earlier in the book, having both accounts allows for options like savings and having your money directly deposited into your account, where you don't have to take out time to go to the bank because the transfer will happen automatically for you.

How to Understand Your Paycheck

Your paycheck will be broken down into different categories. Every paycheck will always have your name, address, and last four digits of your social security number on it, in addition to the information of the company you work for.

Hours: This is the total number of hours you worked for that specific pay period.

Rate: This is the dollar amount you make per hour you work.

This Period: This is the range of calendar dates you have worked during that specific pay period.

Net Pay: This is the amount of money you actually take home once all deductions and taxes are taken from your paycheck.

Gross Pay: This is the amount of money you actually made before taxes and deductions were taken out of your paycheck.

YTD: These initials stand for "year to date." This shows what you have accumulated in total for the year. So for example, your YTD for gross pay may show $2,000, which is showing how much money you have accumulated so far this calendar year.

Current: This shows your total numbers for each specific category on your paycheck for that paycheck period.

Required Deductions Section

Federal Income Tax	This tax rate is the same across the country. This tax is paid to provide for national programs.
FICA Medicare	This tax is charged because it provides medical benefits for people sixty-five and older, certain young people with disabilities, and people with permanent kidney failure requiring dialysis or a transplant.

State Income Tax	All employees must pay this tax. The amount you pay is determined by how much earned income you received.
FICA Social Security	This tax is charged because it provides retirement and disability benefits for employees and their dependents.

Other Deductions Section
This section of your paycheck will include other deductions you may have coming out of your paycheck, such as medical, vision, or dental insurance. In addition, this section will include any retirement accounts you are enrolled in through your employer, such as a 401(k) or 403(b) account, which will be explained in a later module of the book.

Lastly, always be open to learning and expanding your mind and financial skill set. There are always opportunities to learn and expand your knowledge. As part of your basic necessities skill sets, you must continue the growth process by completing tasks, such as investing your time into reading, listening to podcasts, attending workshops, finding a financial guru you can go to and seek advice from, and sharing your knowledge with friends, family, neighbors, and anyone who will listen.

What Is Generational Wealth 101?

On Your Journey ...

What do you aspire to pass down in your family line? To whom?

_____

_____

_____

Reflection Time

Why Is Generational Wealth Important?

_____

_____

_____

_____

_____

_____

Our Family ... Our Future

Generational wealth includes financial assets, such as property, investments, money, or anything with a monetary value, that you pass down from one generation to the next. In addition, it is important to pass along financial education, values, and good habits as part of the process. The best way to begin building generational wealth for you and your family is to start as early as you can, and the best way is by first educating yourself on what it means to have financial wellness. Then, when you educate yourself, keep sharing what you know with your siblings, parents, friends, neighbors, and other family members.

How to Build Generational Wealth
1. Invest in your child's education.
2. Invest in the stock market.
3. Invest in real estate.
4. Create a business to pass down.
5. Take advantage of life insurance.

How to Pass Generational Wealth
1) Write a will. This provides specific instructions on your last wishes and assets. You can map out specific instructions for your children's care. You can also list your financial assets to make it easier for your family members to locate them. When you don't have a will, you leave the decision up to the state when it comes to your children, property, and assets.
2) Set up a trust. A trust, commonly referred to as a trust fund, is a legal entity you can use to hold and transfer assets to your beneficiaries. It is another option to consider for parents of minor children.
3) Name account beneficiaries. To ensure that your assets pass down to the beneficiaries of your choice, it is sometimes as easy as naming specific beneficiaries for each account. Naming beneficiaries can save your loved ones a lot of time and energy in the event of your death, especially if they are adults.

The Wealth Journey
(Module 2)

On Your Journey ...

If you could create a business, what kind of business would that be?

_____

_____

_____

Reflection Time

Why Do We Need Investments?

_____

_____

_____

_____

_____

Ways to Build Wealth 101

Wealth	versus	Active Income
Wealth is an accumulation of assets and property over time.		*Active income* is an amount of money you make in a certain time period, such as your salary or paycheck.

RIB Formula

The key to building wealth is by starting the wealth-building process as early as you can. One way you can begin building wealth is by following the RIB Formula. Aim to position yourself to always have your money working for you to generate more money. Just like our bodies need our ribs to protect our hearts and lungs, we need to allow our money to work for us through real estate, investments, or business income.

R   Real Estate

I   Investment Accounts

B   Business Income

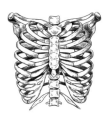

Passive Income Is Key

Passive income is income earned regularly with little to no effort. Initially you may have to put in a little effort or invest money to get the process started. However, it positions a person to have *financial independence* and will *create financial freedom and time.* Passive income is a great way to receive income to use toward paying down debts too.

Examples of Passive Income
- rental property income
- business income that does not require active participation

We all have to start somewhere, such as working a job. However, keep in mind your income from a job depends on you showing up every day and performing a task in order to receive a paycheck. Your income can be limited to the hours you work, your health, and your age. Promotions or raises are nice, but the reality is sometimes that can be dependent on your supervisor's perception of you. *Jobs don't create financial freedom. They create financial dependence.*

Assets   versus   Liabilities

Assets are things or items a person or business owns.	Liabilities are things a person or business owes.
Examples • cash • real estate • investments • funds in a checking or savings account • jewelry and antiques (value has to be verified) • vehicle (depreciating asset)	Examples • personal loans • real estate mortgages • credit cards • student loans • car payments • unpaid taxes

Plan for Your Future *Now*

What Is a Custodial Roth IRA (Individual Retirement Account)?

This is a retirement savings account that allows for tax advantages that you can start now to plan for when you retire. You may be thinking, *Retirement?* But yes, you need to plan and start the process as early as possible. This account can be opened by your parent, other family members, or friend on your behalf until you turn eighteen, if you have earned income.

Earned income is a W-2 job or income from a self-employment job such as babysitting. Once eighteen, the account is transferred to you. Encourage your parents or guardian to set you up with a financial planner and/or advisor to discuss a financial plan for your future.

Success task: Follow the bucket strategy below. This is another way you can understand what it looks like to invest money into a Roth IRA account.

The Bucket Strategy

Bucket 1
Your Contributions

1) Your monthly contribution will be deducted from your or your parents' bank account.
2) This is the money you are personally contributing to your retirement account monthly.
3) You are paying taxes now on every contribution. You often hear people refer to your contributions being made as "after-tax" or "post-tax" dollars.

Bucket 2
Your Wealth

1) Your money inside bucket 1 is being invested into different stocks or companies you have ownership in.
2) All the gains or wealth being built in bucket 2 are growing tax-free.
3) More time means more time for your money to grow.

What does this mean for you?

When you retire, you will receive all of your money tax-free. This means you don't have to pay taxes on any of your money you collect at retirement. You will collect all of the money from bucket 1 (your contributions) and all of the money from bucket 2 (your wealth), and it's all yours to keep!

Did You Know?
- You can pull your money out as early as age fifty-nine and a half years old.
- You can you use your money for qualified education expenses, such as college tuition, penalty free, but the distribution (money received) will be taxed as your income.
- If you have had your Roth IRA account for at least five years, you can pull up to $10,000 over a lifetime, tax and penalty free, to purchase a home as a first-time home buyer.

What Happens to Your Money in the Bank?

Your money grows at .01–.03 percent *return on investment (ROI)*. To keep it simple, ROI is the *profit* you make as a result of the money you've invested. So what does this mean? At the end of the month, if your savings account at the bank has $500, multiplied by .01 percent ROI, your gains or wealth at .01 percent is $5 for that month. As mentioned earlier in the book, we all need some money in the bank for an emergency fund, but the key to building wealth is investing your money into things where it can *grow* and earn a higher ROI.

Having your money in a Roth IRA compared to just sitting at the bank will allow for your money to grow at a higher ROI, and your money will generate wealth over time.

Always seek planning from a financial advisor first.

Success Check-In

Schedule a time to speak with a financial planner about a custodial Roth IRA. What did you learn?

_____

_____

_____

_____

_____

Notes

_____

_____

_____

_____

_____

The Credit Journey
(Module 3)

On Your Journey ...

Do you pay people back when you owe them money, or do you choose not to?

_____

_____

_____

Reflection Time

Why Is Having Good Credit Important?

_____

_____

_____

_____

_____

_____

_____

_____

Credit Basics 101

What is a credit bureau?

Credit bureaus are simply agencies that collect data from lenders from accounts you have, such as your credit card or a personal loan. They compile data from your credit accounts using your social security number or identification number and form credit reports to give to lenders so lenders can determine your creditworthiness. There are three credit bureaus that lenders use: Equifax, Experian, and TransUnion. Credit bureaus don't make the decision to approve you or not. For example, if you apply for a car loan or credit card, the decision to approve you for the loan or not is strictly up to the lender.

Types of Information the Bureaus Collect
- debt collections
- bankruptcies
- credit account information: payment history, date account opened, balance of account, date of last activity, high balance on account, credit limit on account

Our Nationwide Credit Bureaus

Equifax
https://www.equifax.com/personal/
(888) 548-7878

Experian
https://www.experian.com/
(888) 397-3742

TransUnion
https://www.transunion.com/
(800) 916-8800

Is It Accurate or Not?

The reality is credit bureau reporting agencies can make mistakes by reporting inaccurate information on your credit reports. *The Fair and Accurate Credit Transaction (FACT) Act* allows you to have *one free* credit report from Equifax, TransUnion, and Experian each year. You can access your free credit reports through www.annualcreditreport.com. If one finds inaccurate information on a credit report, one can make a dispute to request that information be removed from the report and/or corrected.

Make it a habit to pull your credit reports at least one time a year.

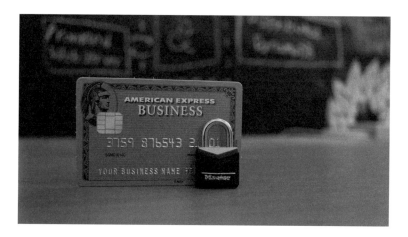

Credit Score Factors

Your Credit Score

A *credit score* is a prediction of a person's behavior and creditworthiness. Your credit score can range from as low as 300 to 850. It is best to aim for a higher credit score because this will result in making it easier to qualify for a loan and receive better interest rates or loan terms. Each credit bureau has a different credit score, so yes, you have more than one credit score. Credit scores are calculated based on the data being collected. Credit scores can differ depending on the scoring model, the type of lending you are requesting, and/or just simply the day it's pulled.

The Breakdown of Your Credit Score

The Data Used To Calculate Your Credit Score

Inquiries
10.0%

Payment History
35.0%

Credit Utilization
30.0%

Length of Credit
15.0%

Credit Mix
10.0%

What Is Affecting Your Credit Score?

❏ **Negative Information**

Negative information are accounts not in good standing that are reported to the credit bureaus. Negative information will affect your overall credit score and will stay on your credit report for up to *seven years.* Examples of negative information are bankruptcies, late payments, collections, foreclosures, and repossessions.

Make a note that chapter 13 bankruptcy can stay on a report for up to seven years and chapter 7 bankruptcy for up to ten years before it is removed from your credit reports.

❏ **Payment History**

Payment history accounts for 35 percent of your credit score. Make it a good habit of paying your bills on time, before or by their due dates. If you absolutely have to pay a bill late, make sure you make the payment before it is *thirty days* past due. When your bill is thirty days past due, it will be reported to the credit bureaus as thirty days past due and will negatively affect your credit score.

❑ **Inquiries**

Inquiries account for 10 percent of your credit score. Anytime you apply for credit, you will receive what is called an inquiry on the credit report that is being utilized. Inquires will stay on your credit report for *two years* before they fall off your credit report. What you need to know is that there is what we call a *hard pull* and a *soft pull*. A hard pull is when your credit is going to be pulled by a lender, and it will impact your credit score. A soft pull is when your credit is pulled by a lender, but it will not impact your credit score.

❑ **Credit Utilization**

Credit utilization accounts for 30 percent of your credit score. Credit utilization looks at how much you're spending based on the available credit you have on an account. Always aim to keep account balances at *30 percent or lower*. For example, if a person has a credit card with a $5,000 credit limit, then they should never spend more than $1,500 of the available credit limit.

❑ **Credit Length**

Credit length accounts for 15 percent of your credit score. Credit length is showing your overall credit history, or you could think of it as your credit experience. What is the longest account someone has had compared to their shortest account they have had? The key is to never close accounts on your credit such as a credit card, unless you absolutely have to. When you close accounts, it can negatively affect your credit score. If a person does decide to close an account, they should always close the account they have had for the *least* amount of time so they can still maintain some credit history.

❑ **Credit Mix**

Credit mix accounts for 10 percent of your credit score. Credit mix is looking at the *diversity* of accounts among your credit report. Having a good credit mix, for example, would be having a variety of accounts, such as installment accounts, an automobile loan, a mortgage loan, and/or revolving accounts (credit cards).

Tips to Improve Credit

- o Pay your bills on time, *before* thirty days past due.
- o Pay student loans or look into forbearance or deferment options.
- o Don't ignore paying medical bills; make arrangements.
- o Apply for credit only if you need it.
- o Keep credit card balances below 30 percent.
- o Have a good credit mix (i.e., auto loan, credit card, mortgage loan).
- o Pay down revolving accounts.
- o Open a secured credit card with your bank if you need to establish credit.
- o Become an authorized user to establish credit from the benefit of someone else's credit.
- o Minimize your debt; always aim to pay debt off as soon as you can.
- o Monitor your credit regularly.
- o Practice responsible spending habits; spend what you can afford.
- o Utilize a credit identity monitoring service.

Your Credit Character

Your credit should be taken seriously. Credit is not about getting a limit to spend on purchasing all the things you want, going on shopping sprees, or vacations. Displaying credit character is to show your history of being responsible with credit and financially reliable. Always make healthy choices when it comes to your credit, and don't apply for it if you don't need it.

Did You Know?
You can become an *authorized user* on someone's credit account as early as age thirteen years old, depending on the creditor. By doing this, you can position yourself to begin to establish all the areas of credit, as mentioned above, to create your credit profile and a credit score. Keep in mind that when choosing someone's account to be authorized on, we want to make sure this is a person who displays excellent credit character.

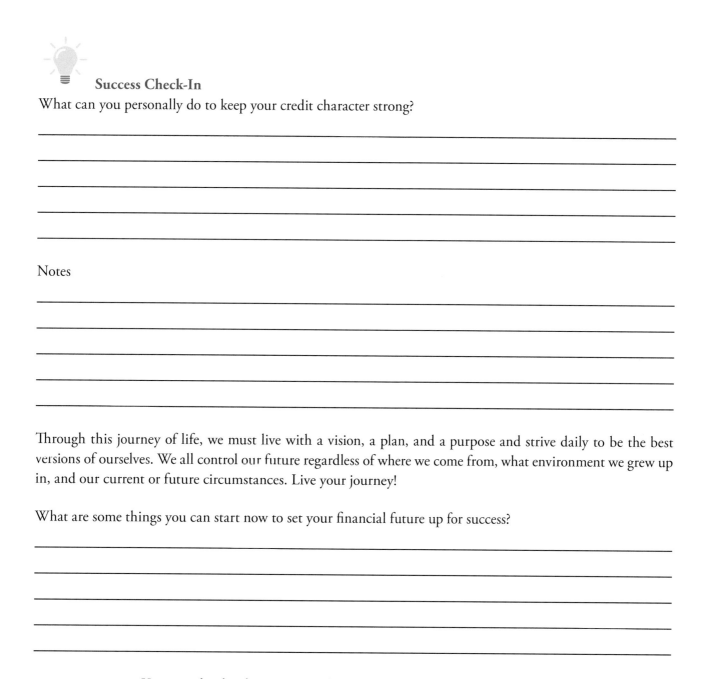

Success Check-In

What can you personally do to keep your credit character strong?

_____

_____

_____

_____

_____

Notes

_____

_____

_____

_____

Through this journey of life, we must live with a vision, a plan, and a purpose and strive daily to be the best versions of ourselves. We all control our future regardless of where we come from, what environment we grew up in, and our current or future circumstances. Live your journey!

What are some things you can start now to set your financial future up for success?

_____

_____

_____

_____

_____

You must be the change you wish to see in the world. (Mahatma Gandhi)

References

Chen, J., February 15, 2003, "Passive Income: What It Is, 3 Main Categories, and Examples," https://www.investopedia.com/terms/p/passiveincome.asp#:~:text=According%20to%20the%20 IRS%2C%20passive,now%20more%20accessible%20than%20ever.

September 9, 2020, Consumer Financial Protection Bureau, https://www.consumerfinance.gov/ask-cfpb/what-is-a-loan-estimate-en-1995.

September 12, 2017, Consumer Financial Protection Bureau, https://www.consumerfinance.gov/ask-cfpb/what-is-a-closing-disclosure-en-1983/.

N.D., Consumer Financial Protection Bureau, https://www.consumerfinance.gov/owning-a-home/loan-options/fha-loans/.

Daugherty, G., February 27, 2022, "Generational Wealth," https://www.investopedia.com/generational-wealth-definition-5189580.

Escalante Troesh, J., May 2018, "Build a Budget in 15 Minutes. Purposeful Finance," https://www.purposefulfinance.org/home/articles/the-15-minute-basic-budget?gclid=C jwKCAjw4ayUBhA4EiwATWyBrqS0kaLBEzAxyh5k5LnV5exHysxDFM05DBwnW_ HfRRhXgpVMJ9ugShoCO7gQAvD_BwE.

N.D., Federal Trade Commission, https://www.ftc.gov/.

Goff, K., 2023, "What Are Assets, Liabilities, and Equity?" https://www.bankrate.com/loans/small-business/assets-liabilities-equity/#examples.

Hayes, A. (March 8, 2023). "Liability: Definition, Types, Example, and Assets vs. Liabilities," https://www.investopedia.com/terms/l/liability.asp.

Kagan, J., December 29, 2021, "Active Income: Overview, Examples vs. Passive Income,"
https://www.investopedia.com/terms/a/activeincome.asp#:~:text=Active%20income%20is%20
income%20received,net%20earnings%20from%20self%2Demployment.

Lake, R., January 1, 2023, "Can You Open a Roth IRA with Your Child?"
https://www.investopedia.com/open-roth-ira-with-your-child-5220429.

Mitchell, C., October 28, 2020, "Personal Financial Statement: Definition, Uses and Example,"
https://www.investopedia.com/terms/p/personal-financial-statement.asp#:~:text=Assets%20
include%20the%20value%20of,%2C%20unpaid%20taxes%2C%20and%20mortgages.

Ramsey, D., n.d., The Seven Baby Steps: Dave Ramsey,
https://www.ramseysolutions.com/dave-ramsey-7-baby-steps.

Ramsey, D., April 13, 2022, How the Debt Snowball Method Works,
https://www.ramseysolutions.com/debt/how-the-debt-snowball-method-works.

Strain, N., January 25, 2022, "Can I Use my 401 (K) to Buy a House,"
https://www.investopedia.com/ask/answers/081815/can-i-take-my-401k-buy-house.asp.

Thoma, S., n.d., "The Four Uses of Cash,"
https://www.edwardjones.com/sites/default/files/acquiadam/2021-02/IPC-8343-A.pdf.

Treece, D., 2022, "What Is an Appraisal Contingency?"
https://www.forbes.com/advisor/mortgages/what-is-an-appraisal-contingency/.

2022, "What Affects a Credit Scores?"
https://www.experian.com/blogs/ask-experian/credit-education/score-basics/
what-affects-your-credit-scores/.

October 17, 2022, What Is a Credit Score?
https://www.consumerfinance.gov/ask-cfpb/what-is-a-credit-score-en-315/.

N.D., What Is a Credit Bureau?
https://www.equifax.com/personal/education/credit/report/what-is-a-credit-bureau/.